Pakistan

Kaghan Valley

Stephen Platt

www.leveretpublishing.com

Pakistan: Kaghan Valley
First published - October 2017
Published by
Leveret Publishing
56 Covent Garden, Cambridge, CB1 2HR, UK

Camp in Bedadi en-route to Balakot

ISBN 978-1-912460-11-3

Pakistan
Kaghan Valley

Emily So and Steve, Naran. Kaghan Valley 5 June 2006

Pakistan 2006

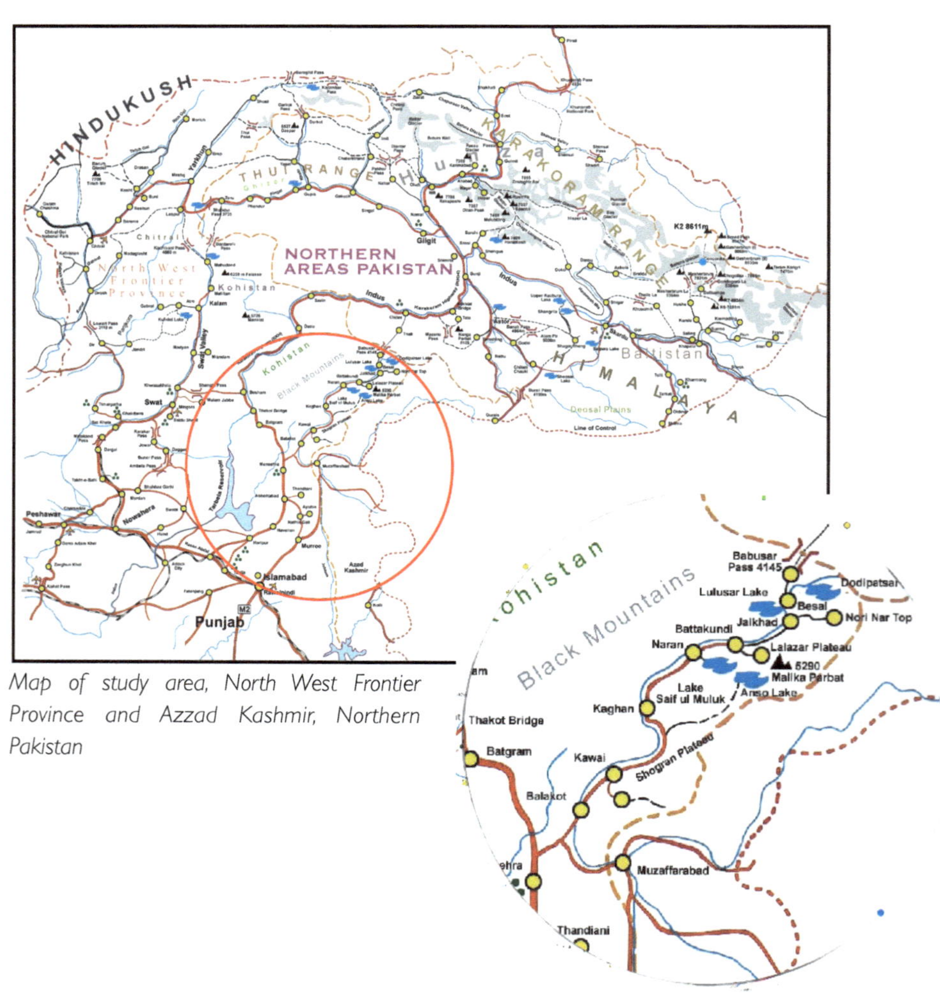

Map of study area, North West Frontier Province and Azzad Kashmir, Northern Pakistan

Introduction

This is a report of a field trip with Emily So of Cambridge University to the areas affected by the Pakistan earthquake of 8 October 2005 in May and June 2006.

The trip had two objectives. The aim of the trip for Emily was to conduct a survey of survivors of the earthquake about their injuries and to relate these to the buildings they were in as part of her PhD. My aim was to shed light on the factors affecting long term recovery after major disasters. We were accompanied by Dr John Beavis, a Consultant Orthopaedic Surgeon from the UK, by Professor Amir Khan from the University of Peshawar and his team of 6 post graduate interviewers and by Mubashar Lone a business man from Burnley, UK who working with the Kashmir Charitable Trust (KCT). We interviewed people in Islamabad responsible for coordinating relief and reconstruction and visited the areas affected by the earthquake. On our rest day we drove up the beautiful Kaghan Valley as far as we were able.

Kaghan Valley February 2013, 8 years after the earthquake

Understanding some of the issues faced by survivors of the earthquake was a powerful experience for us both and we were treated with the warmest hospitality and generosity by everyone we met in Pakistan.

In Muzaffarabad in Azad Kashmir we saw many signs of commerce returning, rebuilding and life getting back to something approaching normality in the town centre. We visited projects to provide work and training – in computer science and sewing. In the suburbs of Chella Bandi and Mera Bandi, a mile or so from the centre, we saw disturbing indications that long term help is not arriving. People need money and advice to rebuild their homes and the injured need long term treatment. For example, we talked to a secondary school teacher who has a deep infection and desperately needs remedial surgery, and to a young engineer who is still traumatized after the loss of many members of his family.

The International Aid organizations and the Pakistan Government, once they realized the scale of the disaster and had cleared the roads, were well organized and provided effective relief. But on all our travels we saw few signs of them working eight months, although we did see lines of white UN Jeeps

Muzaffarabad, earthquake damage

with their satellite aerials waiting for reassignment.

In Balakot, in North West Frontier Province, the fault line had passed through the main bazar and despite almost total destruction, commerce had returned, debris was being cleared and materials – stone, bricks, and steel reinforcing rods, were being recycled and stacked and reconstruction had begun. Although the Government was adamant that Balakot would be relocated 20 km south, given its strategic position at the foot of the Kaghan valley, the town will most likely be rebuilt on the old site despite any plans to move it.

Many families here as elsewhere, were still living in tents. They badly needed money to be released to rebuild their homes and clear advice about recommended construction. In the villages of Kawai and Garlat, on the outskirts of Balakot, many people lost their lives and 120 children died when their school slid from a ridge a thousand feet to the valley floor. The high death toll of amongst children is a scandal and the level of destruction of schools and hospitals is preventable.

Balakot, earthquake damage

Islamabad

Tuesday, 30 May 2006
I only dozed on the plane because I couldn't get comfortable in the tight space. A young Pakistani woman in the row in front of us was looking after two small girls, one a baby with big round eyes; she managed them wonderfully.

Wednesday, 31 May 2006
It was already hot at 5am when we got off the plane and were met by a man with a sign saying Shalimar who whisked us off to our hotel. Even at this early hour the streets were thronging with people going to work – nearly all men, in the ubiquitous long shirts and baggy pants, the shalwar-khameez, and the traffic was a dodgem of bashed yellow taxis, motorized rickshaws and smoke-belching trucks.

I got into bed and fell asleep until 1pm local time and then had lunch in the hotel with Dr John Beavis, a trauma surgeon who helped Emily on her

Rawalpindi

previous trip in November, before setting off for our first interview with the World Health Organisation (WHO). John has a delightful way of negotiating. He asks the price and then promptly doubles it. This way of offering a bung we name a 'Beavis' and manage to negotiate the hire of the taxi for the next two days for 5,000R (£50) a princely sum here. WHO were in a sector of town accommodating diplomats, international companies and wealthy locals that seemed alien to the rest of Pakistan.

Rachel Lavy, Co-ordinator for WHO in Islamabad, was a competent, modest person who had taken charge of the health cluster responsible for coordinating all medical aspects of the relief effort. She had been running a polio eradication campaign to get all children in the country immunised when the earthquake struck and she took charge of medical relief. Today, coincidentally, we read in the local paper that someone in the provincial government is opposing her polio campaign on grounds that it affects male virility.

Rachel recounted the relief efforts to us and also what is being done at the moment in Pakistan, 8 months on from the earthquake. The tents survived reasonably well after the winter as they were lucky in that this year,

Our taxi and chauffeur for two days,

they had a relatively mild and short season, although in the higher reaches, temperatures were still way below freezing. The government had decreed that all camps be closed by the end of March but the organisation set up to guide reconstruction and rehabilitation (ERRA) has yet to finalise the building codes and designs! Over 2 billion USD have been donated to Pakistan by international development funds but on the ground, none of this money was in evidence. She said the Pakistan Ministry of Health was overwhelmed and WHO had brought in people to provide support. We overlap with UNDP, who provide shelter and camp management. Since April ERRA, the Earthquake Reconstruction and Rehabilitation Authority, has taken over from Federal Relief Commission, which was responsible for immediate relief. ERRA is military-led and holds the reconstruction purse strings. NGOs are encouraged to liaise with ERRA, which can cause delay, but is a good discipline.

Their engineering report on building failure in hospitals and clinics showed that cross bracing and opening lintels were skimped and they failed because they were badly built. The earthquake happened during Ramadan. In general the men were sleeping at 9am on a Saturday morning and children were at

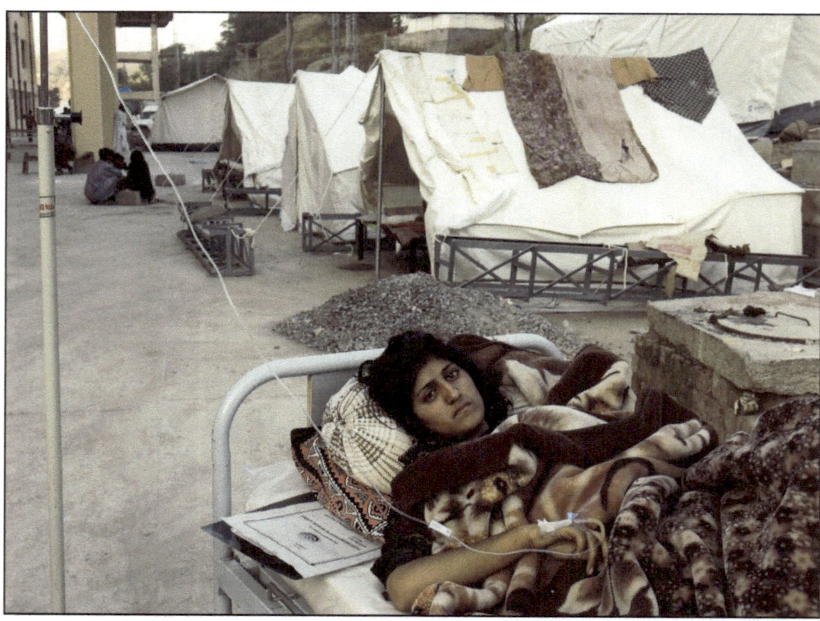

.A woman receives medical care outside a hospital in Muzaffarabad. Half of all health facilities in affected areas were destroyed, (WHO/Christopher Black)

school which explains the high death toll. There was no accreditation and approval scheme for volunteers. Having said that, some outfits were excellent. For example, INSURAG, an international rescue organization, formed by firemen after the 1988 Armenian quake, provided a very good response, similar to the WW2 heavy rescue units.

Rachel's partner Kasim is Anglo-Kashmiri. In Kashmir, people in the affected areas are intelligent and resourceful, they will make provisions for the coming winter and will cobble together shelter at any cost to stay on the land because they don't want to be in camps in the valley. Land is everything, she says, and the Government fed people's fears that India would use the disaster as a pretext to invade. Many people in the North West Frontier Province (NWFP) are still living under a feudal system and have never owned land. Over time the system is gradually changing and people are able to buy land. Bargaining power of workers is also a factor. It has been decided at the highest level that Balakot will not be rebuilt since the whole region is prone to landslides.

Muzaffarabad people are Kashmiri. Some work in Islamabad; our houseboy is from a village near Muzaffarabad, said Rachel. As soon as he heard about

Dr John Beavis, a trauma surgeon who helped Emily on her trip in November, 2005

the earthquake he took a bus to check on his family and had to walk nine hours to reach his village because the road was blocked. He found his house flattened and that he lost 15 members of family. He walked back to get help. We told him to bring his family but, despite everything, his parents wouldn't leave, so he bought five tents to house them. Finally we got them here a but they were utterly miserable and felt they had deserted their community, so when his mother felt better, they went back.

It is a remittance economy with many family members working in the UK and Middle East. Many Kashmiris moved en-mass to the UK in the 1950's. Azad Kashmir means Free Kashmir. There is some local autonomy and local administration and it is treated with kid gloves, like an autonomous province, by Islamabad who are worried about secession. The seat of government in Muzaffarabad was destroyed and the local government administration decimated. Members of the federal government are fighting amongst themselves and this disempowered the Kashmiri government. ERRA set up provincial bodies responsible for administration – PERRA at province level and SERRA at state level, but both are very weak still.

Pakistani contruction worker in Saudi Arabia. In 2015-16 Pakistani workers sent remittances of $20 billion, nearly 1/10th of GDP. (Express Tribune July 16, 2016)

Thursday 1 June

We spent the day talking to doctors at the Pakistan Institute of Medical Services (PIMS) who had treated most of the patients from the earthquake. Anwar ul Haque, Professor of Pathology and coordinator for all earthquake relief medical teams, was a delightfully warm, compassionate thoroughly competent man. He reported that all government buildings collapsed whilst most private non-domestic buildings did not, the reason being substandard construction due to corruption. I'm a very open person and am not afraid of speaking out, he said.

The Margalla Towers residential block that collapsed in Islamabad brought the disaster home to people. It was Ramadam and everyone was in high spirits. The earthquake happened at 9am but the first victim didn't arrive until 3 pm because the road from Islamabad was blocked. Within hours of learning of the quake we had organised blood transfusions, extra beds, and broadcast on the radio and TV for volunteers and all was ready by the time people began to arrive. It was like the first drops of rain, then a deluge. The first relief trucks left around midnight to go to the affected area and it took them 10 hours.

Margalla Towers, Islamabad

Voluntary relief organisations were not that well organised and we established a register of volunteers who were assigned according to abilities and needs to avoid chaos. Maybe there were some bad people. There are stories of abduction of children, of well-connected people posing as doctors, and of people trying to recruit young women for the sex trade. We took a strong stance on this. Mobile phones were crucial in helping coordinate people and equipment. The international NGOs thought of us as crooks, but something we learnt about our own people; they did the right thing and responded with unbelievable charity, for example, a catering company supplied food and a mobile phone company offered free service. Endless lines of trucks kept arriving from Karachi and the south with aid.

The hospital here was initially overwhelmed with fractures of all kinds, including head injuries. Many died, including many women who rushed inside to protect children. In general they are at home more than the men. This means that most of paraplegics are young women. The Pakistan Ministry of Health did a good job, funds were freely available and we were dispatching 3-4 vehicles a day laden with medical equipment. Community centres were converted to medical facilities, with beds and food and PIMs provided medical staff. I was appointed as the overall coordinator because my department, pathology, is much freer in crisis to take this role. We performed 200 operations a day and arranged training sessions for volunteers. There was a good team from Britain, also Cubans, Koreans, Russians and it was obviously easier with English speaking teams.

People were arriving with nothing – no shoes, no underwear, no money. We arranged packs for people and photographs of people admitted or treated were displayed outside the hospital. The police cooperated and, in general, families were reunited quickly. People live in close extended families and we didn't need genetic testing and it was exceptional, after a disaster like this, that more people were not lost. Immediate relief was excellent, aided in part by the morality and spirituality of Ramadam and Anwar was very moved by the extent of human charity from all over the world. A lot of young people volunteered.

Long term we didn't need loans from the IMF of $4million and the extra burden of interest and poor people will be paying for this. Pakistan already spends 40% of it's GNP on repaying debts and this loan puts us further into the red. There is no clear indication of where the money will be used and we now know the loan was unnecessary given the generosity of the international community. The government has created a dependency culture. Many of the people in Kashmir have families in England and donations to rebuild the hospital in Muzaffarabad are still pouring in. Kashmiri people are naturally independent and don't need pampering by government. They had good medical provision in Kashmir, but their doctors and nurses were pampered by Government and developed slack habits over a long time and so when the earthquake struck they failed to respond effectively. They are tough people in the remoter areas of NWFP, they are self-sufficient and well fed. They have plenty of food and it was wrong to dislocate them. Men come down to Islamabad to work and send money back. But the country is so corrupt; with Afghanistan, we produce 70% of world's heroin.

Reconstruction was beginning to go well and there was no need to demolish entire homes that only had slight damage. Compensation is delayed, it would be much better to use family self-help than government aid and crooks are taking advantage. Even people with minor injuries are exaggerating to get

People were brought to hospital any which way. *https://www.islamichelp.org.uk*

more compensation. The Government had still not started reconstruction eight months after the quake and children have not been going to school for a whole year and it will be hard for them to get back into a routine. There was a severe lack of heavy lifting and cutting equipment. The British team did a good job, but took 3-4 days to arrive and were unable to bring heavy equipment. Initially the Government shut-down the mobile phone network for security reasons.

We were with Dr Anwar 4-5 hours and at one point he and his colleagues left for prayers. His office was open house to people coming and going: students and young doctors following his diagnosis on a microscope with additional eye pieces and servants and secretaries bringing papers to be signed and food and drink. He invited us to lunch and began to talk about Muslim civilization, the Koran and religion and became quite passionate and a little didactic –zeal mixed with a deep humanity.

We next went to interview Andrew McCloud Relief to Transition Advisor to General Nadeem, Head of the Earthquake Reconstruction & Rehabilitation Authority (ERRA) with rank of Brigadier General. Andrew was energetic,

Dr Anwar ul Haque, Professor of Pathology PIMS, coordinator for all earthquake medical relief

confident and proud of his achievements in gaining a position of influence with General Nadeem and in coordinating the relief effort. Rachel said he was the driving force in managing the 'clusters' that were set up to coordinate the relief and in getting things done. He had been chief operations officer at UNHCR when news of the earthquake broke and had jumped on a plane. He was at a meeting with General Nadeem at the beginning and had pulled him aside and asked to speak with him in private. He told him he had been in the Australian military and that a friend, a Brigadier, had said the worst thing was that no one told you when you were wrong. General Nadeem asked him what he meant and Andrew told him that he would do that for him, for example he couldn't just task NGOs as he'd been doing in the meeting they'd just been in.

We asked him about his home and family and he opened up with a story about his upbringing and his estrangement from his elder brother and how General Nadeem had tried to arrange a romance for him with another Australian aid worker and we had a discussion about the merits of arranged marriages. Andrew described the current debate in ERRA about what types of construction will be approved – traditional or concrete? He asked us if

General Nadeem Head of EERA, Chikar Rural Health Center Inauguration, 19 June 2007

we were prepared to stay on for three or four months and advise ERRA. He said that General Nadeem is very enlightened, for example he wants to focus educational funding on girls, but there is a lot of uncertainty still and a need for good communication for people not linked to media.

The disaster had one positive outcome, it opened up Kashmir. Prior to the earthquake, only seven people had been allowed into Indian Kashmir and during the relief operations there was a most remarkable absence of bad will. The International Red Cross did a good job and it was impossible to distinguish between national and international response because of good coordination. We spent the evening at the French club in the diplomatic quarter of the city, a heavily guarded complex, housing all the international embassies. We were going to meet Rachel and Andrew McCloud for dinner. As we drove into the complex, security got tighter and there were road blocks every 50m. At the end of this strange road was the British embassy with its 4 tiers of barbed wire and next door the American embassy, built like a fortress with double walls. Over dinner Rachel mentioned that inside there were cinemas, restaurants and shops and that the Americans who are posted to Pakistan never actually leave the compound and get their food and water flown in.

Diplomatic enclave, Islamabad

Abbottabad and Thandiani

Friday 2 June

The Daewoo bus to Abbottabad was smooth, comfortable and air-conditioned and the stewardess had a beautiful mellifluous voice. We are met by Amir Khan, Professor of Urban Planning at Peshawar University and his driver in a Willeys Camioneer, the 'Khan-mobile'. Emily and I were whisked off and after dropping our belongings at the Shelton Hotel we had a light lunch at the Government guest house where Professor Khan and his team are staying. I mentioned that I would like to see the hill station near Abbottabad called Thandiani and, since it's a half day on Friday, Professor Khan thinks it's a good a idea to take the whole team there.

It's a nice drive up a paved road through pine woods and meadows to a hill-top with bungalows left by the British. We wander around enjoying the cool air and the views and go for a short walk along the gently rising ridge to an empty bungalow and well-clipped lawn.

Thandiani hill station near Abbottabad with Professor Khan and his team

The story on the ground was different from the somewhat rose-tinted view we'd been given by medics and government officials in Islamabad. Villagers were still in tents, which were filthy and shabby or metal huts which were intolerable in 40 degree temperatures. Some of the richer people, especially in Kashmir where there is a lot of remittance money from the West, have begun rebuilding themselves but there is confusion as to how to build and whether the government will compensate them. We visited places where local NGOs were still evident but the international community were thin on the ground.

We heard harrowing stories of a little boy who refused to leave his father's grave left one of the interviewers devastated and a family in Kawai that lost 6 out of 8 members. The collapse rates of schools and health centres was shocking with over 75% collapsed. In one of these villages, a school was sited at the top of a ridge and all 170 pupils were killed when the school slid down the steep hillside. Again and again we saw preventable deaths, poor building quality and a lack of guidance and awareness from government that had so far failed to transfer little of the donated money into rebuilding lives and livelihoods.

Professor Amir Khan and his team of interviewers from Peshawar University

Muzaffarabad

Saturday 3 June 2006

Sitting around in the living room of the rest house talking with Professor Khan and his team of four young men and two women interviewers it quickly became apparent that they know what they are doing.

The main street through the town was bounded by a vertical wall of river boulders which by some miracle hadn't collapsed. Some tents were still in evidence, but everywhere there was a huge amount of rebuilding. Commerce was thriving, teeming humanity throng the streets, bumping and jostling into us as we squeeze past, trying to avoid being mown down by taxis and trucks. Tractors crawl along in the heavy traffic hauling heavy duty trailers full of grey sand dug from the bed of the river Jeelum.

Mubashar Lone, our contact from Burnley for Kashmir, took us to a hotel to meet his friend, a Kashmiri surgeon who worked for the Kashmir Charitable Trust (KCT). The hotel was huge with a wide terrace overlooking the river and there were signs of cracking in the walls that had been patched and a major

Bustiling commerce in main street of Muzaffarabad

repair and refit programme was underway.

We had decided to use Chella Bandi, a suburb of Muzaffarabad about a mile from the town centre, as our pilot study area. Many of the houses were damaged and some had collapsed entirely and the interviewers were dispatched in pairs along different side streets. Many people were still in tents and those that owned their houses and land were camped in the cleared ruins of their homes. Those from the area of landslide, which completely wiped out their community, were living in tented camps.

We were shepherded around by a couple of young coordinators from KCT who have been working with the families here. They introduced us to a young man in his late twenties called Rajah Kalim, from one of the richest and most influential families in the community whose uncle was the chairman of this area. He invited us to see his destroyed home and described the moments when the earthquake struck and many members of his family were killed, how you couldn't see for dust and how he ran from the house when the quake started. His brother died protecting his mother by covering her with his body. He was very emotional and kept repeating himself. I can't prepare

Rajah Kalim, engineer traumatised by his father, brother and uncle, who escaped by running out of his house in Chella Bandi, a suburb of Muzaffarabad

my mind about what to do, he said. We were well-settled, established people, we had a comfortable life. The temporary shelter in the Turkish prefab they had been assigned was too hot, he said and the aid agencies didn't understand the realities on the ground. The Government should explain what people need to do, he said, they have offered 25,000 R compensation to people, which isn't enough. There has been too much delay. They announced that they would have a plan and would issue advice in a week, then two weeks, then nothing, no action at all and people are finding this so hard. The international community needs to help by creating work and then people could help themselves. First thing the government needs to assess whether it is possible and safe for people to return and rebuild and then they need to provide advice on how to rebuild safely, or help them to migrate to other, safer places. 80% of people are mentally disturbed. What can I do?

My cousin was trapped near Chella bridge. He rang his boss on his mobile and told him where he lived and that he was trapped. The rescue team with heavy machinery came after three days. It was awful; fathers having to cut the legs off children to get them out. We were reliant on self-treatment for my

Interview team setting off in Chella Bandi

mother and sister. My auntie was treated in Islamabad. She couldn't walk, but got there herself. The home next door was built by my cousin who is a civil engineer. It was undamaged, whilst our house collapsed completely. I believe that the basic thing is to create awareness of good design amongst people so they will insist on good construction.

We are taken by Mubashar to meet people at the Kashmir Charitable Trust (KCT). Dr Mohsin Shakil, Consultant Urologist from the Bradford Medical Mission, was involved in making a database of survivors with 10,000 photos. Some children were stolen and taken to Pakistan, he said and we don't know what happened to them, they could be dead. It was completely lawless for the first week and even the President said "help yourself" and it was a credit to local people that we managed. We enrolled young people and set up a routine of checking on every area. There was no medical treatment for the first two days and a medical team from Mirpur was first to arrive and had to work in tents until first field hospital arrived on the tenth day. They did 500 amputations on first day. After two or three days the roads were open and people were moved out of the area for treatment.

Dramatic land slip on the other side of the valley from Muzaffarabad

Amir Khawaja, KCT coordinator, said that when the earthquake struck he called his friends and talked about what they should do. The first thing was to establish security forces because people came from outside the area to rob and kidnap children and the police force was out of action. We started a basic computer course with the idea of establishing a computer company to give more advanced training but the government levied 40,000 Rupees duty on the computers we were given from the UK.

In Chella Bandi we visited a high school teacher in his forties who was lying on a bed being massaged by his wife. He said he was teaching and his hip was dislocated trying to save children. He'd had 11 operations, all of which have failed to fix it and, according to John, he has deep infection which must be treated by a specialist remedial surgeon. He had sought for help from the authorities who said he could go back to the government doctor in Muzaffarabad, but he 'doesn't know his arse from his elbow'. He has also had to buy a temporary home for 108,000R that he had erected on the site of his house. His wife was giving him physiotherapy. We joked about his smoking. A sweet poison, he said. A good friend, and a bad enemy.

Dr John Beavis talking to young men in Chella Bandi

That evening we had a discussion about village of Bedadi. Professor Khan had got the most animated we had seen last night in discussion with Navid and Tajir, the two men from Peshawar who have been working with John Beavis and his charity Ideals on rebuilding the village of Bedadi. They have been planning to build houses for forty families while Professor Khan said they should provide only the land and basic services. Navid seemed taken aback and began a discussion. Clearly they intend to build. He said they had looked at nine sites and selected one. They intend to provide 21/2 marlas for each house (a plot 16.5 x 16.5 ft). Professor Khan said this was too small for a rural home in which people store their wood for fires, the straw for animals, and where will they keep their chickens. Navid and Tajir reacted strongly by saying that the government recommended 21/2 marlas and wouldn't fund more than this and anyway they couldn't afford twice as much land and still build the houses. Professor Khan said that they shouldn't be building the houses, that it was better for people to do it themselves, that building the houses created dependency. I said that this was the main way poorer people housed themselves in South America.

Children of Bedadi where Ideals, a charity founded by John Beavis was helping rebuild homes

Professor Khan said that it was important that the site be near the main road and that anywhere along the Mansehra road would allow small shops and businesses to prosper and the income could be invested in community facilities. John, Navid and Tajir had problems adjusting to the idea of not building the houses and seem to have created a dependency by going to the village many times. Would the land owners at Bedadi already have begun to rebuild if John hadn't intervened, I wondered? Sensitive to the implied criticism, Navid said, they had just finished distributing food. Professor Khan said that the best thing to do would be to distribute funds to households in instalments and, if they used the money to rebuild, they would get more funding. You have to understand this country, he said. Individually families can be trusted to do the right thing, but collectively, for example giving compensation to a whole community, doesn't work; someone would steal it all. I had a chat with John the following morning. He understands the sense of more land, but is still thinking that they need to build the houses. I said that it might be better to let people build their own. At first it would be anarchic and ugly, but in the end the village would be more interesting and beautiful through organic growth.

Family camping out on the collapsed roof of their house by the main road

Balakot

Sunday 4 June
Mubashar said he is coming to Balakot with us because the people we want to see won't be there and places are closed. I've never been, he says. I want to see what's happening on the other side (in the North West Frontier Province). Maybe we can go to Bedadi, and if John is putting in £20K we could put £10K and do more.

The main street in Balakot is teeming with people selling and buying, pushing past each other on the crowded sidewalk. Nearly all the buildings are collapsed but shop-keepers have erected rude stalls in timber and tin. There are shops selling cement, corrugated steel sheets, plywood sheets and timber and everywhere there are people recycling building materials. There are small saw mills by the side of the road with portable band saws and generators and there are big stacks of mud red brick and concrete blocks, piles of recycled steel rods and men are using simple bending frames to straighten them.

The wheat harvest is in and the patch work of tiny fields are pale yellow

Commerce returning to main street in Balakot

with stubble. Bearded old men are scattering seed for the next maize crop and spreading piles of manure.

The road bridge was damaged in the earthquake and there is a Bailey bridge and a ford. The road climbs steeply and soon we are high above the river on a switch-back road, narrowed by landslides to a single lane. Children are going to the UNICEF tent school and lines of Jeeps and transports are moving people along the Kaghan valley.

Gujar herdsmen bring their animals from the plains south of Islamabad to high summer pastures at this time of year and we have to squeeze past herds of goats, sheep, cattle and horses. These people look very hardy and carry their world with them and their fortune is in their flock. They come from the Punjab and once ruled the whole of northern India. The men have beards and woollen hats and the women wear gold ear and nose rings and colourful scarves. The older men are dark and fierce with beards. They tend to rest during the day, then in the evening they start off again and travel through the night when the traffic is lighter. Did they suffer less in the quake than agriculturalists? They speak Gujari and our driver is from this tribe. They

Ford across the river in Balakot

used to stop at our village to rest, says Professor Khan, and I like speaking their language.

Gujar tribesman moving herds up to high summer pastures in Kaghan valley

They have dogs for security, Professor Khan says to protect their flocks from wild animals – tigers, lions and snow leopards and from thieves. There are tigers in Nathagali and they had to shoot one recently. The herdsmen usually kill one of their flock when they know tigers are about, but this one developed a taste for humans and they had to kill it.

The tribesmen whack their beasts out of the way with switches. I am in the outside seat and as we squeeze past I look out of the window, hundreds of feet down to the boiling river. The driver, Mazhar Ali Zeb, from Ibrahim's taxis, is fantastically good, but we are inches from the edge and it is all so unstable after the quake. Above us, for hundreds of feet, are steep tottering slopes of scree with boulders as big as houses perched ready to fall. I begin to understand why Professor Khan intersperses nearly every sentence with Insha'Allah – God willing.

At Jared there is a makeshift roadside cafe, the plastic table and chairs sitting inches deep in a stream. The owner waves us in, but we are on a mission to reach Kawai where we will hire a jeep to continue. The valley is wooded with tall stately pines and the slopes on the far side of the valley are green and

Footbridge over the gorge of the Kunhar River, Naran Valley

undamaged whilst on our side, where the new road has been widened six or seven years ago, all is devastation and ugliness. The steep slopes are fenced into tiny plots and there is stubble from a recent harvest. Professor Khan says the area is famous for its delicious potatoes. In the distance we can see snow covered peaks; Not Nanga Parbat, that's further up the valley a day's journey away and we probably won't get that far, but these are 5,000 metre peaks and their glaciers reach the valley floor. The river looks cold and deadly, the flow is very fast and we debate whether anyone could raft or canoe down it.

Kawai lost over half its population and the survivors were traumatised and literally didn't know what to do. 120+ children were killed when the school slid a thousand feet down the mountain side and was buried under a rubble mountain that blocked the stream and we heard about many families who had lost all their breadwinners and about children who been orphaned. When we asked about their hopes and fears they said that their hope was in God and their fear was that the earthquake would come again. There was a clear difference between people who owned their homes, who now camp out on their land in shacks and tents and are beginning to rebuild, and tenants who are living in tented villages.

Terraced plots in Naran Valley

Kaghan Valley

We soon leave the main highway and head up a side valley to Shogran, an alpine style resort in meadows and pine woods at 3,000m. The older timber bungalows are undamaged while the newer concrete hotel complex is badly affected, and parts are collapsed entirely. We change to the jeep we hired in Kawai and go on to the Alpine meadows of Paya but the road is blocked by a fallen tree, so we get out and walk the last bit which is more pleasant than being rattled around in the jeep and we saunter up the track between the trees. The tiny restaurant at Paya has been destroyed, but the owner has

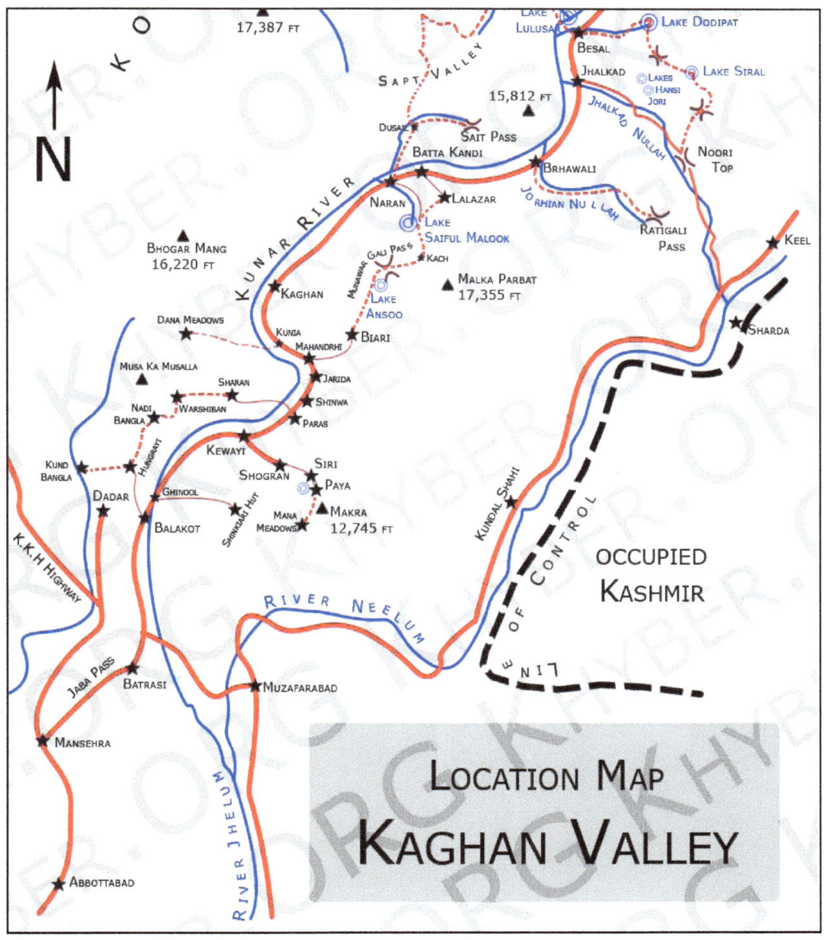

Section of Kaghan valley from Balakot to Naran

Emily, Amir and Mubashar in Shogran

Lake Paya, Shogran

rebuilt his kitchen and there are rude benches to sit on and we stop for a rest and Mubashar and Amir order lunch. Emily and I are keen to walk on, but Professor Khan persuades us to stop and just taste. So we wait. It is pleasant looking across to the meadows and the lake and the food when it comes is quite delicious – dahl and a vegetable curry that Emily says tastes like fresh crab, all eaten with the fingers and naan bread, almost the best food we have on the whole trip, and cooked in a shack on a wood fire.

We have just an hour for a walk as Professor Khan says it is a long journey back and we have promised to take the team of interviewers out for dinner in Abbottabad. We set off, taking a path to the lake rather than the main track that winds round the mountain and crosses the watershed into the Neelum Valley before dropping down to Muzaffarabad. Our driver says it would take three days to walk there. I'd like to do it, but another day. The grass is cropped short, and we scramble through white peonies to the roadway. There are wild iris and the sky is blue with big thunder clouds to the north west and we wonder if, like yesterday, we will have a storm. We can see Malka Parbat (5291) to the north, but not Nanga Parbat as the guidebook promised. Too soon we reach a point

Makeshift kitchen in Shogran

Lunch with Amir and our amazing driver Mazhar Ali Zeb

Malka Parbat (5, 296m) the highest mountain in Kaghan Valley

where we will have to return. We go on a few hundred yards and are rewarded with a view of nearby Mount Makra (3885). The slopes are still snow-covered.

It's companionable sauntering back and neither of us have felt the altitude and it is delightfully cool after the heat of the plains. At the rest house we have green tea and set off with Professor Khan and Mubashar for the jeep. Emily and I continue walking rather than climb aboard the jeep but after a while Amir says he's worried about the time and we climb aboard for a bumpy ride back to Kawai. The interviewers are waiting for us by the side of the road in Kawai and are upset and disturbed by what they had heard from the villagers.

We get back late to find that Major Munir has invited us to dinner. His research is on women's roles in Pakistan today, nevertheless we eat apart from the women. The major tells funny stories about his early training, but either the students are shy or they aren't as funny as he thinks. I could hear Emily in the other room talking about football to the children because the women were talking Urdu. The food was good and Professor Khan piled up our plates.

High point on our walk above Shogran

Monday 5 June

We get another early start and repeat our journey of yesterday, this time without Mubashar, who drove last night to Lahore. The interviewers have gone back to Chella Bandi today. Professor Khan has decided they need a break after yesterday. They are going to visit the upper part of the community they didn't reach before. The Kaghan Valley is the old Silk Road from China to India and Arabia that crossed the high Himalayas. It goes from Balakot in the south to Chitral and Gilgit in the north and the epicentre of the 2005 earthquake we have come to research was just north of Balakot. This is the mythic North West Frontier, home, in imagination at least, of armed Pakistani tribesmen and site of the Great Game. Amir Khan was as excited as I was at the prospect and Emily, having satisfied herself that the survey was proceeding well, was keen to go too. My *Pakistan Handbook* had said this was a beautiful area, but Emily thought it might have been destroyed in the quake. The whole valley is owned by one man and his property stretches for 130 miles and the people living here are tenants and have been badly hurt by the quake. Many of the stone houses have collapsed and we see lots of tents. There are quaint square pagoda style

We have to wait for some hours while they clear a way through a recent avalanche

Digger clearing recent avalanche

Road cleared and we can progress

houses which may be holiday homes of the rich. We drive to Kawai and then we take a jeep to Naran. We hope to reach a beauty spot – Lake Saiful Maluk.

The valley is very beautiful, narrow, steep and wooded with a patchwork of pasture and tiny ploughed terraces awaiting replanting. There is a lot of damage and the trees are scarred from stone fall. The road is still blocked in places and the army is working on glacial slides.

We had to queue with many Jeeps and trucks and we were waiting in the queue when we saw a well dressed man struggling across the glacier, his shoes covered in mud. He was having difficulty walking, maybe he'd had a stroke, but despite this he was determined to find out what was happening. We invite him to have tea from a roadside stall and he tells us his story. His father was head of Pakistan International Airlines (PIA) and wrote books on aeronautics. His wife arrives, she's been waiting in the car and is a little annoyed at having been left so long. She says there is a saying, if you stand too long you grow roots. It seems unusual for Pakistan that she is so outspoken with strangers. Then we hear she lived in Germany for many years, as a translator and then ran a clinic giving Raike massage. She tells Emily that they were childhood sweethearts,

Newly wed couple we met while waiting to get through to Naran

We finally reach Naran

Young men are playing cricket in the main street of Naran

Fresh trout supper out of tradional newspaper wrapping

Classic painted pakistani truck wedged against a pick-up

but married other people. Her husband died and she contacted him knowing he was divorced and they have been married six months. Her two grown up children did not approve, but now, seeing them happy, they have come round.

We finally reached Naran where a group of young men are playing cricket in the street and in the event there wasn't time to reach the Lake Saiful Maluk. Although we fail to reach the lake, we achieve our secondary objective – a delicious meal of fresh caught river -trout! Professor Khan has been thinking about this meal since he was last here in 1976, before any of the tourism and hostels. We find a man who says he can get us fresh trout and after some time he returns looking furtive with his hands across his chest. Once out of sight of the road he unzips his fleece and reveals the fish. There are police and government officials about and it is prohibited, he says. We drive up the valley and return to delicious brown trout out of newspaper. Professor Khan shows me how to eat trout with the skin – crispy and tasty. The trout were introduced by the British who brought eggs from Scotland. He knows about this from the English from the British High Commission who have been here for the fishing.

We climb aboard a jeep and our driver and Professor Khan chat while Emily and I are thrown about on the back seat – most of the other Jeeps fill up with as many as 10 people so they are usually packed tight. From Kawai the road is much worse since they haven't scraped down to the road surface and there are huge random boulders to negotiate and stream beds to cross. Every few minutes we meet oncoming traffic or fight our way past a slower vehicle. The drivers are fantastic, especially the ones driving the huge Bedford truck, old and belching black smoke, but they seem to get everywhere a jeep can. The truck beds are locally made, high sided steel structures painted all over in colourful murals and Arabic prayers, winking coloured rear lights and chains hanging from their rear bumpers like exotic necklaces.

Islamabad

Tuesday 6 June 2006

We have an appointment with General Nadeem at ERRA that has been arranged by Andrew McCloud and Rachel Lavy. We get the 9:30 bus from Abbottabad having been seen off royally by Amir and the Ibrahim taxi drivers. The journey is equally smooth and we are able to get a rest before taking a taxi to the guest house. We have time for a sandwich and make notes about what we'll say to General Nadeem. The plan is for Emily to describe the project and for me to give a summary of our observations. In the event General Nadeem is unavailable. He's preparing an important presentation for President Mussaref. We meet Rachel at reception and are met by Major Mushtag Hussain who introduces us to Lt Colonel Abid Hussein. He says that we should give our report to him. He ushers us into a grand conference room and we squeeze in past gilt chairs and sit down. Rachel says she is from WHO and introduces us as her guests. The Colonel contradicts her, saying we are his guests and the guests of Pakistan.

Emily explains the purpose of the survey and I ask him if he has time to hear our summary report. He says yes of course, if we have come all this way he has more than enough time to hear us out. I pretend to be speaking for Professor Khan, and indeed most of the points I make are things he has suggested. I realize that it is almost impossible for a man like Amir, a civilian, to get an audience with ERRA.

We talked to people in their homes in Chella Bandi, Muzaffarabad and in Garlat-Kawai, Balakot and the interviews we'd had with doctors and relief workers in Islamabad and Muzaffarabad. Reconstruction is going ahead – commerce is returning, people are starting to rebuild their homes and local NGO's are rolling out model housing designs but most people we spoke to were confused about what to do and were waiting for promised government assistance and advice. There was an urgent need for infrastructure reconstruction and financial support of individuals. Professor Khan's advice about distributing assistance is that the home is very important to Pakistani families and he believes that very little money would be wasted or go astray. The cost of building materials has nearly doubled. Cement has gone from 250

Rs a bag to 400 and the cost of blocks has similarly increased. Advice about recommended construction forms would ideally be graphic since most people rebuilding are not trained construction workers.

We understand that it has been decided re-site the town of Balakot, but commerce has returned and the old town is thriving and the main street is thronged with new shops, including those selling building materials.

As well as rebuilding homes and public buildings, livelihoods are also important. We saw a number of projects by local NGO's in Muzaffarabad aimed at training and job creation. There is also much evidence of post-traumatic shock amongst survivors and a need for specialist therapy.

The Colonel picks up on one or two issues, in particular he is surprised about the cost of building materials and says that the information they have been getting is that there has been little increase in prices and that inflation is under control. He says forcibly that Balakot will not be rebuilt and that any new buildings will be removed.

He asks our opinion of pre-fabrication. The question is in the context of a discussion about rebuilding homes so we understand he refers to houses. We say that independent of what materials or forms are used the important thing is the quality of construction. We had seen many instances of buildings that had failed of all types of construction, and evidence that well-built buildings survived. It was difficult, we said, to control for quality, especially in joining pre-fabricated panels and that in any event pre-fabrication would only have a very marginal impact, given the scale of rebuilding required. It only became apparent later that he was referring to proposals to re-build medical facilities using pre-fabricated concrete panels. He ends the meeting abruptly and we leave feeling dissatisfied.

We have one last interview with Maryam Mallick, a doctor and coordinator at WHO who has been responsible for founding and running rehabilitation centres for earthquake victims. We began immediately collecting data, she said, to assess the magnitude of the disaster and we visited hospitals and camps. In all there were 741 spinal injuries and 713 amputees. These include all kinds of amputation from small finger to whole leg. With proper documentation the total could be 900-1,000, but not any higher. But this is still a surprisingly low figure given that over 100,000 were injured during the earthquake. Surprising those with head injuries suffered no neurological deficit, but then most patients with head injuries didn't survive.

Patients were moved from the earthquake zone to Peshawar, Islamabad and Lahore for treatment and 21 patients were sent to UAE. 65% of spinal injuries were women who were at home, many of them living in poverty in poorly built houses. Most of the men were working away from home. The way patients were moved had a major impact on the severity of spinal injury. Patients should have been immobilised during transport, but this didn't happen and many people suffered incomplete paralysis injuries. People reported that, while waiting for rescue, they could move their legs. For example one man, an academic, reported that he was dragged down stairs from first floor and then along the road to the transport. Rescuers thought they were doing good. There were many complex fractures, survivors had to wait 7-8 days for medical attention and by this time gangrene had set in and a lot of amputations had to be done because of infection. Field hospitals managed to control infection once people arrived but those coming late from remote areas were obviously more badly affected.

There was also a wide-spread misconception that lots of artificial limbs would be needed. 1,000 arrived as international aid. Shops opened selling prostheses for $4-500. It was thought that this would be very profitable. But limbs need to be custom fitted and you have to take a cast of the stump to get exact contours. There were many agencies working in provision of prostheses, for example, ICRC provided a 100 bed orthopaedic prosthetic workshop

Lake Saiful Maluk, Photo by Miriam Malick

in Abbottabad. Limbless Foundation Handicap International were based in Mansehra.

There were no checks on qualification and training of volunteer doctors and the capacity of the hospital system was inadequate; they were flooded with patients and there was an acute shortage of everything – of nurses, doctors, equipment and supplies.

Spinal injuries need specialised care but patients were scattered all over the place in different hospitals and wards, on verandas and in corridors, with no special care. WHO immediately built a 100 bed prefab clinic and started bringing patients together for treatment. We organized 100 medics, 50 psychologists, and shifted all the patients under one roof. We set up three centres: 2 in Islamabad and 1 in Rawalpindi, plus a military unit. There were about 100 spinal injuries amongst military personnel that were treated separately. It was a holiday for the army and many young soldiers were asleep in their barracks. The army hasn't released the exact number of casualties; they estimated 2-3,000, but the true figure is likely to be much higher.

There were also many nerve injuries – foot crop, hand drop. People often waited 3-4 months before seeking medical help, wondering why they hadn't got back full use of their limbs and assuming that they would eventually get better naturally. There were also problems of post-facture contraction – due to lack of movement during splinting and people were not told clearly that they needed to exercise their limbs. Many of these patients now need physio help.

Many spinal patients have bladder/bowel control problems. Literacy level is low and we need to train patients in the use of a catheter. They are told to put it in the bladder every four hours, but they do it every half hour or not for 6-8 hours and have problems. (One man even put his catheter into a Pepsi bottle.

I believe we adopted a well organised approach, she said. We gathered data about the scale and nature of injuries, a spinal unit was built quickly and a workshop established a comprehensive plan for patient rehabilitation. This was one of recommendations of the National Regulatory Authority that got immediate approval. We set up rehabilitation centres in Muzaffarabad and Abbottabad and developed manuals for paramedics and mid-level physios. We started training workshops for occupational therapists to help make patients independent. We had only one occupational therapist in the country before earthquake but we had lots of expats coming back to help and we organised a certificate course. We developed a strategy to reintegrate patients into community and devised a manual for the families and for the community to help them understand how to help people integrate back into society. This is part of a comprehensive community based rehabilitation programme which includes primary level community workers.

On our return Professor Amir Khan wrote the following:

The geography of the mountainous region combined with political tensions and an overall lack of preparedness meant that many people, especially in poor rural communities, did not receive the help that they desperately needed for days or even weeks. The people affected by the earthquake were vulnerable when the disaster struck. Winter was beginning to descend on the Himalayas, and it was the Islamic month of Ramadan, when many Muslims observe a fast between sunrise and sunset. The dispute over territory raised questions about governmental responsibility, and international aid was slow to arrive. Western countries were accused of suffering from "compassion fatigue" following the Boxing Day Tsunami of 2004 and Hurricane Katrina in the summer of 2005.

The Kashmir earthquake affected conflict-stricken cities that the people of other nations had no connection with (they were not holiday or business destinations) and a lack of accessibility meant that images of the aftermath were not transmitted straight away. Although awareness and fundraising campaigns led by British-born Pakistanis were profoundly influential during Kashmir's time of need, the British government was criticised for not doing enough to help. Many people felt that they should, for example, have sent more Chinook helicopters to help aid reach isolated mountain villages, rather than have these helicopters stationed in Iraq, where Britain was at war. It was for these various reasons that the Pakistani government found itself trying to organise a grand scale recovery operation with relatively few resources.

Disasters such as this, where the actions and speed of response of governments, armies, NGOs and ordinary citizens can save lives on a grand scale, can be mitigated by learning from past mistakes. By analysing what happened in Kashmir from 2005 onwards other regions can become more prepared for disaster.

Discussion

Reasons for building failure

The main reason so many people were killed or injured in the 2005 earthquake was building collapse, and irrespective of building type, materials or site conditions, the main reason for building failure was poor construction. We saw examples of buildings that had survived of all types of construction – traditional and modern, timber and stone, or concrete and brick. Whilst close by, buildings of the same construction type had collapsed. The difference was, quite evidently, poor construction.

Site selection also must play a part. In Muzaffarabad whole settlements had been caught in huge landslip and in Balakot, houses on a ridge above the town had slipped and in Kawai the school had been taken by a landslide. But most of the houses on flat land in Balakot and Chella Bandi, Muzaffarabad, had also pan-caked, the walls collapsing inwards or outwards into rubble leaving the flat concrete roof-slab unsupported.

The wide-spread failure is clearly due to poor wall construction. Typically the

The ground floor of this house pancaked, killing the occupants

Masonry construction with round stones has little resistance to shaking

Poorly constructed concrete column sheers and buckles

concrete columns have no cross bracing and the steel reinforcement is likely to be underspecified and inadequately tied at corner joints. Infill masonry is poorly bonded and not tied to the surrounding concrete frame. We were told that the concrete blocks, which are used for much of the infill masonry, are made with only a tenth of the required amount of cement. Stone masonry is often poorly done with few bonding through stones. Some 75-80% of medical facilities and possibly a greater proportion of schools and other public buildings, such as police stations and local government offices, were destroyed. The WHO engineering report on hospital collapse highlighted lack of cross bracing and inadequate lintel support as two main reasons for failure.

This was all in marked contrast to the few examples of traditional construction we saw using timber posts and beams in the walls and heavy roof timbers supporting a clay roof. Traditional construction relies heavily on large section timber for its strength. The availability of timber is, however, a major issue for the Government and there is acute concern about the extent of deforestation over the past thirty years which has exacerbated the risk of landslides.

We saw a number of small Government tree nurseries in the Kaghan

Traditional timber and stone house is undamaged, Ghanool, Balakot

Valley near Naran. However, there is clearly an urgent need for a much bigger reforestation programme and for the creation of long-term managed forests that could provide a locally grown sustainable supply of timber for construction. This will be a very long-term solution, since trees will take a least fifty years before they can be harvested.

Delay in providing immediate relief

The international aid community and the Pakistan Government eventually did a good job in providing relief but aid was slow to arrive and many people had to wait a week or more. The reasons for the delay were largely due to remoteness, and certainly the areas were blocked by landslides and there was difficulty getting helicopters into the area. But there were other contributory factors. Initially, the attention of the national relief teams was focused on the Margalla Towers, modern apartment block in Islamabad and two key areas of command and control were temporarily disabled by the earthquake. Pakistan has a military government and the army suffered massive casualties. This diverted attention and disrupted the chain of command. The general collapse of public buildings in the affected areas also meant that medical staff and civilian

Bedadi Village, Mansehra

authorities in the affected areas, including the police, were out of action.

There was a general lack of preparedness for dealing with this scale of disaster. There was a lack of trained rescue teams with heavy equipment. Volunteer rescuers, typically surviving neighbours and family, were quite naturally untrained and ill-equipped to drag people out of collapsed buildings and render appropriate aid: for example the need to immobilize people with back injuries before moving them.

Long-term reconstruction

Local people are rebuilding their lives and reconstructing their homes. But to date, this process is largely self-helped rather than government inspired. The UN Sphere guidelines to long-term reconstruction suggest three key indicators to recovery: return to home, livelihoods and transport links. Everywhere we went there was evidence of people returning home and starting to rebuild. Most of the large camps have been disbanded and many people are camping out on their own plots. Building materials are being recycled and sand and gravel is being hauled from river beds to make concrete. We were unable, however, to establish if any of the houses that are being rebuilt in and around

Bedadi temporary camp

Balakot are of sound earthquake resistant construction.

The town centres of Mansehra, Muzaffarabad and even Balakot, which was totally destroyed, were bustling with people and commerce. The rubble had largely been cleared and, in a make-shift way, the shops are getting back to normal. The main roads were cleared and traffic is flowing. Only in the mountains, were the roads are continually re-blocked by landslides and glaciers was road clearance continuing.

But the promised government assistance and reconstruction programme was slow to appear. There is an acute delay in providing advice about approved building methods. Eight months on there was still a debate about recommended forms of earthquake-proof construction. The delay in issuing clear simple advice is causing uncertainty and confusion. Local NGO's are filling the vacuum with their own models and people are starting to rebuild their homes with the materials to hand. Both these outcomes were unsatisfactory and will have produced inadequate or downright dangerous homes. Families badly needed money to be released to rebuild their homes and clear advice and models for recommended construction. This advice needed to have been be given in clear graphical form, on handouts and posters, rather than in complex engineering drawings.

Field survey of survivors

The aim of the survey is to gather information from survivors of the earthquake about their injuries and subsequent treatment, and to relate these to where they were and the type of building they were in when the earthquake struck. This data was used to help devise a method of estimating earthquake casualties in future earthquakes. 531 questionnaires representative of 4,246 individuals were returned in Chella Bandi, Muzaffarabad and Garlat-Kawai Balakot, and 8 other villages in the Kaghan Valley.

Land or houses

Bedadi, is a village on the Karakoram Highway north on Mansehra that was badly damaged by the earthquake, John Beavis and his charity, Ideals, had been working with a local NGO in Peshawar called CAMP to provide forty families made homeless with shelter, clothing and food. It was the intention of these two charities to buy land and build new homes for these people. However, Professor Amir Khan suggested an alternative of providing land and basic services rather than building new homes for the people of Bedadi. Professor Khan said that the main problem with a proposal to build homes was that the plot size of 68 m2 recommended by the Pakistan Government was too small for rural housing. People in rural areas need space to store feed for animals and wood for cooking and heating, as well as space for hens and livestock. Nor did this plot size allow any room for expansion. He cautioned that building homes created dependency and advised that it would be preferable to provide at least twice as much land, together with basic services, and allow people to build their own homes.

In the light of this advice CAMP and the charity Ideals explored the idea of buying more land. Naveed, Chief Executive of CAMP, began working closely with Professor Khan on site selection and a place-making strategy for the new community.

Conclusion

To end on a positive note we saw and experienced wonderful things. Everywhere we were greeted with smiles and offers of tea. On the last day high in the Kaghan Valley, we were stuck in a traffic queue of for 3 hours where the army were clearing an avalanched glacier and were made to wait. All around people were quietly waiting and doing what they could to amuse themselves; groups of men helping each other to fix their vehicles or chatting by the roadside. The community spirit was very evident and is getting most people through the tragedy.

The earthquake claimed the lives of 80,000 people, left over 100,000 injured and made 2.5 million people homeless. But there are some good outcomes. The National Institute for the Disabled have managed, through the help of the amazing Maryam Mallick from WHO, secured funding to increase the number of trained personnel in the public sector from 1 occupational therapist to over 100 doctors, 100 physios and 50 psychologists who are learning from rehabilitation programs in Afghanistan and Nepal.

However, our principal concern was that despite the lessons of poor construction, homes hospitals and schools might not be rebuilt sufficiently better to resist future disasters in this earthquake prone region.

Acknowledgements

The funding for this field trip was provided by the EPSRC. Emily So is a doctoral student at the Martin Centre, Department of Architecture, University of Cambridge and Dr Stephen Platt is Chairman of Cambridge Architectural Research Ltd.

We also received the most generous help and hospitality from everyone we met in Pakistan. In particular We would like to thank the people we interviewed:

People interviewed:

Rachel Lavy, Coordinator, World health Organisation, Islamabad

Anwar ul Haque, Professor of Pathology, Pakistan Institute of Medical Sciences, PIMS

Dr. Syed Fazle Hadi, Consultant Physician and Cardiologist and Head of the Department of Medicine, Pakistan Institute of Medical Sciences, PIMS.

Andrew McCloud, Relief to Transition Advisor, Earthquake Reconstruction and Rehabilitation Authority, ERRA, Pakistan

Naveed Ahmad Shinwari, Chief Executive, Community Appraisal & Motivation Programme (CAMP), Peshawar

Tahir Ali, Programme Manger, CAMP

Dr Mohsin Shakil. Consultant Urologist, Bradford Medical Mission

Aamir Khawaja, Coordinator Kashmir Charitable Trust in Muzaffarabad

Dr Maryam Mallick, WHO Coordinator, Consultant Physical Medicine and Rehabilitation.

Lieutenant Colonel Abid Hussein, Coordinator ERRA.

Field team: Professor Amir Khan, PhD; Ms Shukria Begum, Ms Nadia, Anwar Khattack, Asim Shahkad, M Ijaz, Malik Zada,

Our drivers: Zaim Khan, Mazhar Ali Zeb.

Our thanks and admiration to

Dr John Beavis, Consultant Orthopedic Surgeon and Founder of *Ideals*, and Mubashar Lone, from *Burnley for Kashmir*, who accompanied us in Pakistan.

Professor Robin Spence, Director of the Cambridge University Centre for Risk in the Built Environment (CURBE) and the principal investigator.

www.ingramcontent.com/pod-product-compliance
Lightning Source LLC
LaVergne TN
LVHW052258100826
845147LV00001B/85

* 9 7 8 1 9 1 2 4 6 0 1 1 3 *